WORKBO
WORK!

Preschool-Kindergarten

LEARNING IS FUN

Helena Ann DeLuca

Dorothy-Frances Books®
dfbooks.com

WORKBOOKS WORK!
Preschool-Kindergarten

Published by Dorothy-Frances Books®
First Edition; First Printing
www.dfbooks.com

ISBN-13: 978-0-9997911-3-4
ISBN:10: 0-9997911-3-3

THIS BOOK BELONGS TO:

____

Tips for Parents

There is nothing better than sitting down with your child with a physical book—one that they can write and color in and save for many years to come.

Sit, watch, and enjoy your child's participation as they work their way through the pages of their workbook. Read the instructions out loud to your child as you go through the activity pages. Be sure to praise your child when they get the right answers!

Included throughout the book are various learning activities, including 5 sets each of those activities listed below. There are other fun workbook pages, like learning colors and shadow matching for spatial recognition, too!

Alphabet Letters
Counting Fun
Missing Days
Find the Spy
Teaching Time
Disorder and Disarray
Hide and Seek

Alphabet Letters # 1

Fill in the blank next to the "lower case" letter on the left side caterpillar with its matching "upper case" letter you will find on the right side caterpillar. The first one is done for you.

i	I	D
e	___	J
a	___	G
g	___	O
m	___	A
r	___	M
n	___	E
d	___	H
z	___	Z
j	___	I
s	___	R
h	___	S
o	___	N

Counting Fun #1

Read each question and color the circle next to the correct answer.

Which group shows 5 creatures?

○ 

○ 

○ 

Which group shows 6 creatures?

○ 

○ 

○ 

Which group shows 5 creatures?

○ 

○ 

○ 

Which group shows 5 creatures?

○ 

○ 

○ 

Which group shows 1 antelope?

○ 

○ 

○ 

Which group shows 2 lobsters?

○ 

○ 

○ 

Which group shows 5 creatures?

○ 

○ 

○ 

Which group shows 5 bulls?

○ 

○ 

○ 

MONDAY — TUESDAY — WEDNESDAY — THURSDAY — FRIDAY — SATURDAY — SUNDAY

Missing Days #1

Write the missing days in the blank spaces provided.

1. Saturday   Sunday   ______________

2. ______________   Sunday   Monday

3. Sunday   Monday   ______________

4. ______________   Friday   Saturday

5. Wednesday   Thursday   ______________

Find the Spy #1

Find the spy by coloring the spaces with the following characters: The 1st one is done for you. Use your favorite colors!

Once you have colored all the above character's spaces, the remaining character left in the grid is the spy! Circle the spy from the 3 choices at the bottom of the page, and then color the spy!

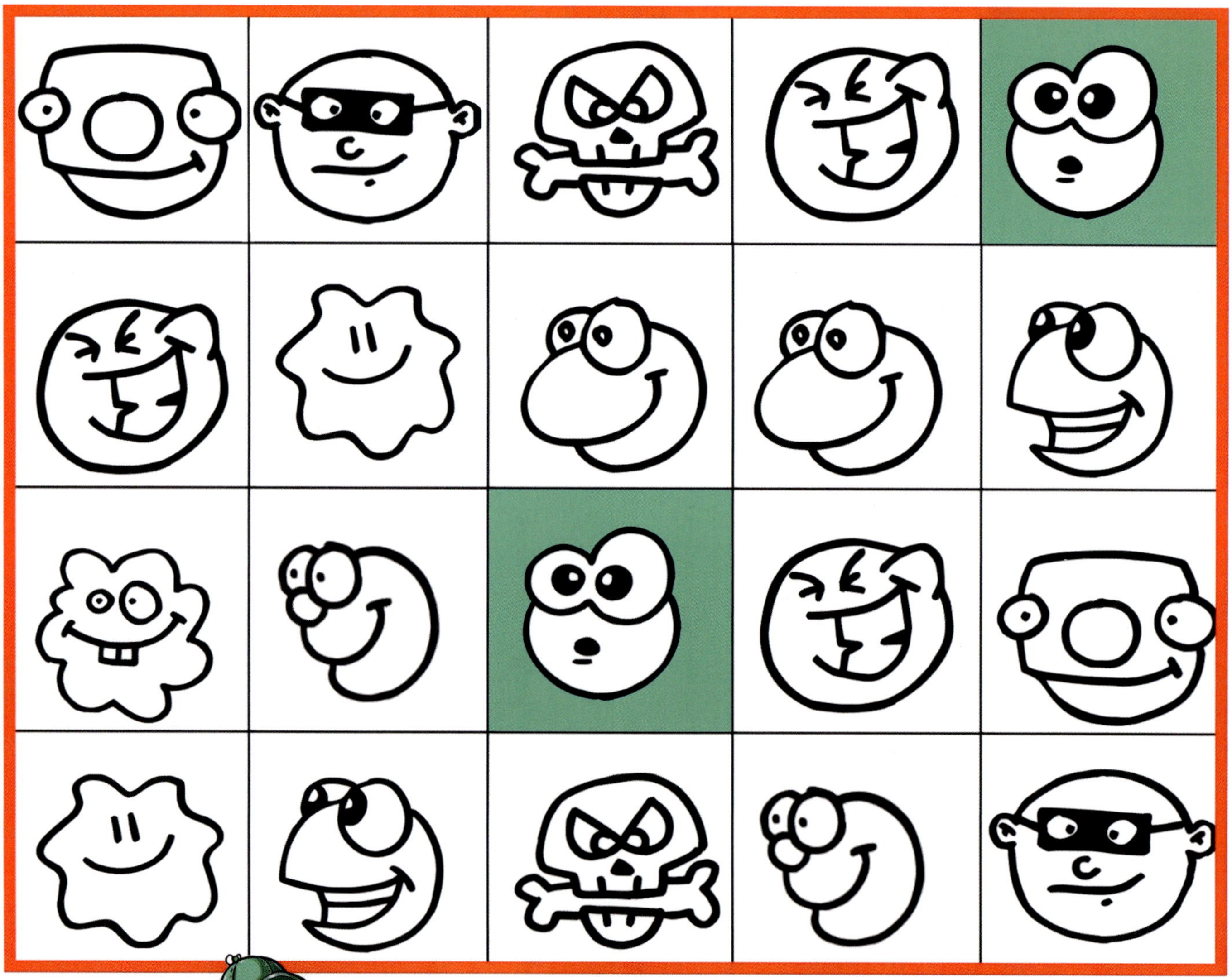

Circle the Spy:

Teaching Time #1

Look at the clock. What time is it? Color in the circle next to the correct answer.

6:00	11:00	3:00	1:00
O	O	O	O

5:00	9:00	11:00	2:00
O	O	O	O

8:00	6:00	4:00	3:00
O	O	O	O

5:00	11:00	12:00	8:00
O	O	O	O

Disorder and Disarray #1

Take a careful look at these two sets of characters. Each side has a character that is not on the other side. Color the **matching** characters—even though they may be different sizes—and find the **unique** characters that are on each side!

Hide and Seek #1

Look for the flower style in the **"Find This"** box. Then look in the **"How Many?"** box for how many to find in the series below. Color the flowers **PURPLE** when you find them! The 1st one is done for you. Look carefully—some of the flowers can look similar.

Find This	How Many?
	5

MATCH THE NUMBER to the number's name!

three

five

one

eight

ten

two

nine

seven

six

four

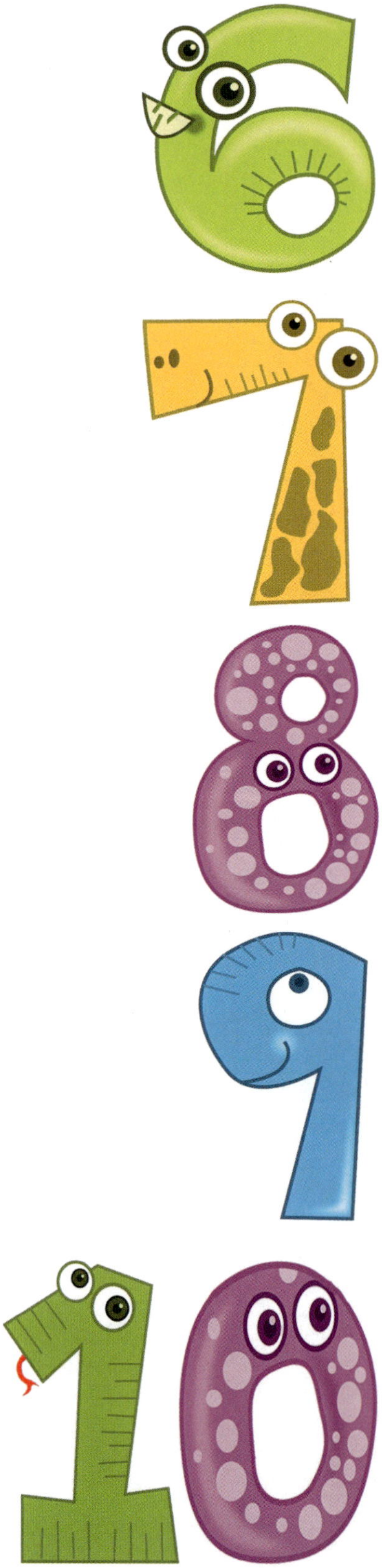

Alphabet Letters # 2

Fill in the blank next to the "lower case" letter on the left side caterpillar with its matching "upper case" letter you will find on the right side caterpillar. The first one is done for you.

Counting Fun #2

Read each question and color the circle next to the correct answer.

Which group shows 1 butterfly?

Which group shows 1 pig?

Which group shows 2 lobsters?

Which group shows 2 creatures?

Which group shows 1 creature?

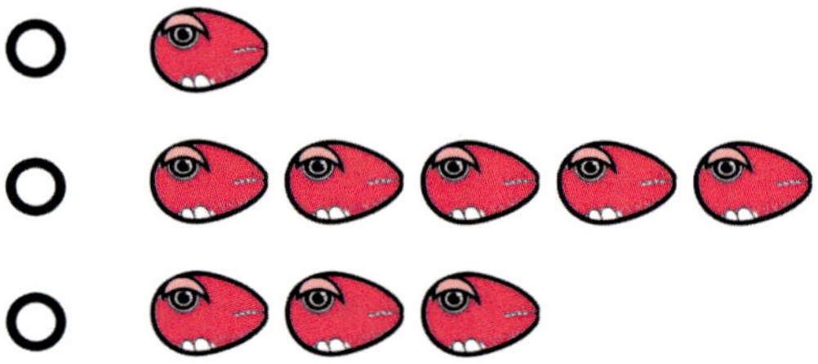

Which group shows 1 creature?

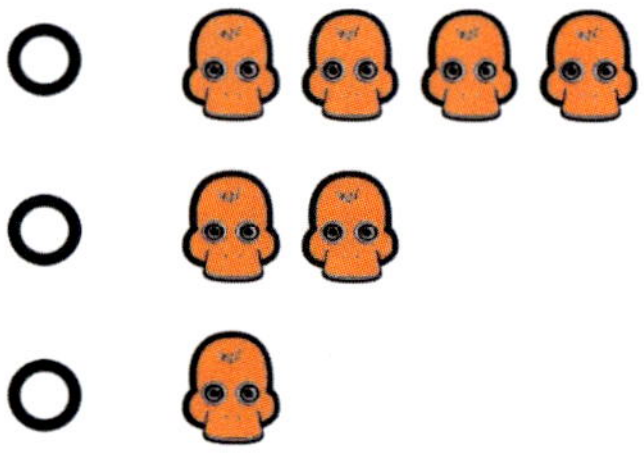

Which group shows 2 bulls?

Which group shows 1 panda?

MONDAY — TUESDAY — WEDNESDAY — THURSDAY — FRIDAY — SATURDAY — SUNDAY

Missing Days #2

Write the missing days in the blank spaces provided.

1. Wednesday Thursday ______________

2. Monday Tuesday ______________

3. Friday Saturday ______________

4. Wednesday Thursday ______________

5. ______________ Tuesday Wednesday

Find the Spy #2

Find the spy by coloring the spaces with the following characters: The 1st one is done for you. Use your favorite colors!

Once you have colored all the above character's spaces, the remaining character left in the grid is the spy! Circle the spy from the 3 choices at the bottom of the page, and then color the spy!

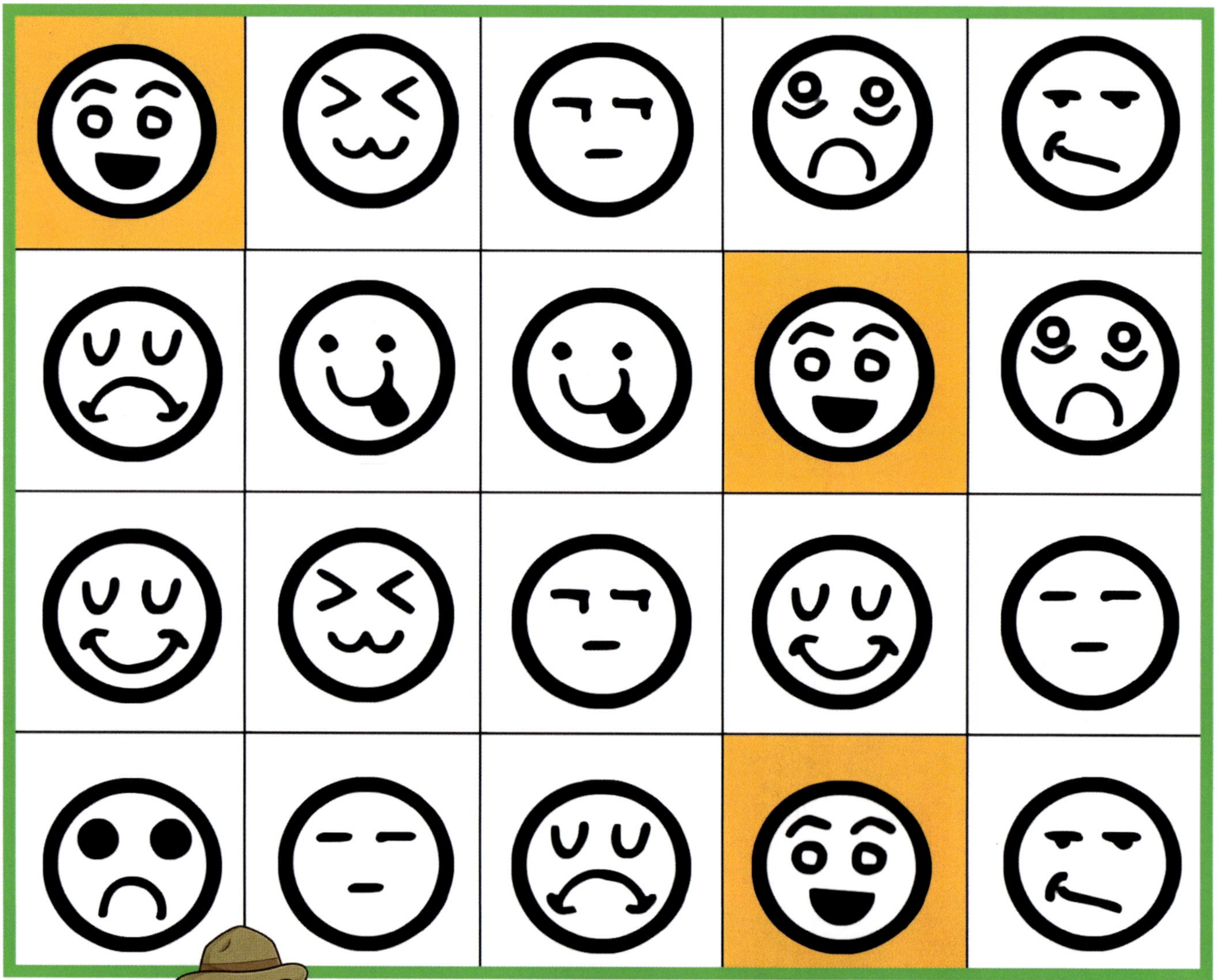

Circle the Spy:

Teaching Time #2

Look at the clock. What time is it? Color in the circle next to the correct answer.

1:00	5:00	6:00	10:00
○	○	○	○

11:30	12:30	4:30	8:30
○	○	○	○

8:00	7:00	1:00	10:00
○	○	○	○

11:15	12:15	7:15	8:15
○	○	○	○

Disorder and Disarray #2

Take a careful look at these two sets of characters. Each side has a character that is not on the other side. Color the **matching** characters—even though they may be different sizes—and find the **unique** characters that are on each side!

Hide and Seek #2

Look for the flower style in the **"Find This"** box. Then look in the **"How Many?"** box for how many to find in the series below. Color the flowers **YELLOW** when you find them! The 1st one is done for you. Look carefully—some of the flowers can look similar.

Find This

How Many?

6

WHAT DOES NOT FIT? Circle the one that's different

1.

2.

3.

4.

5.

Alphabet Letters # 3

Fill in the blank next to the "lower case" letter on the left side caterpillar with its matching "upper case" letter you will find on the right side caterpillar. The first one is done for you.

Counting Fun #3

Read each question and color the circle next to the correct answer.

Which group shows 5 owls?

Which group shows 3 pigs?

Which group shows 1 creature?

Which group shows 2 creatures?

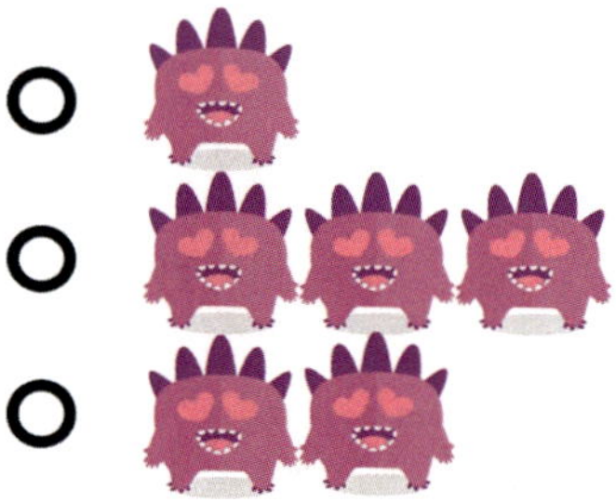

Which group shows 6 horses?

Which group shows 6 creatures?

Which group shows 1 cat?

Which group shows 3 creatures?

MONDAY – TUESDAY – WEDNESDAY – THURSDAY – FRIDAY – SATURDAY – SUNDAY

Missing Days #3

Write the missing days in the blank spaces provided.

1. __________ Tuesday Wednesday

2. Tuesday Wednesday __________

3. Monday __________ Wednesday

4. Thursday __________ Saturday

5. Friday Saturday __________

Find the Spy #3

Find the spy by coloring the spaces with the following characters: The 1st one is done for you. Use your favorite colors!

Once you have colored all the above character's spaces, the remaining character left in the grid is the spy! Circle the spy from the 3 choices at the bottom of the page, and then color the spy!

Circle the Spy:

Teaching Time #3

Look at the clock. What time is it? Color in the circle next to the correct answer.

6:15	9:15	12:15	3:15
O	O	O	O

5:30	6:30	11:30	9:30
O	O	O	O

2:30	8:30	12:30	10:30
O	O	O	O

9:15	6:15	1:15	5:15
O	O	O	O

Disorder and Disarray #3

Take a careful look at these two sets of characters. Each side has a character that is not on the other side. Color the **matching** characters—even though they may be different sizes—and find the **unique** characters that are on each side!

Hide and Seek #3

Look for the flower style in the **"Find This"** box. Then look in the **"How Many?"** box for how many to find in the series below. Color the flowers **PINK** when you find them! The 1st one is done for you. Look carefully—some of the flowers can look similar.

Find This

How Many?

7

Match the Colors

YELLOW

RED

BLUE

GREEN

ORANGE

Color each of the boxes with the matching color!

Yellow

Orange

Red

Green

Blue

Alphabet Letters # 4

Fill in the blank next to the "lower case" letter on the left side caterpillar with its matching "upper case" letter you will find on the right side caterpillar. The first one is done for you.

Counting Fun #4

Read each question and color the circle next to the correct answer.

Which group shows 1 tiger?

Which group shows 4 antelopes?

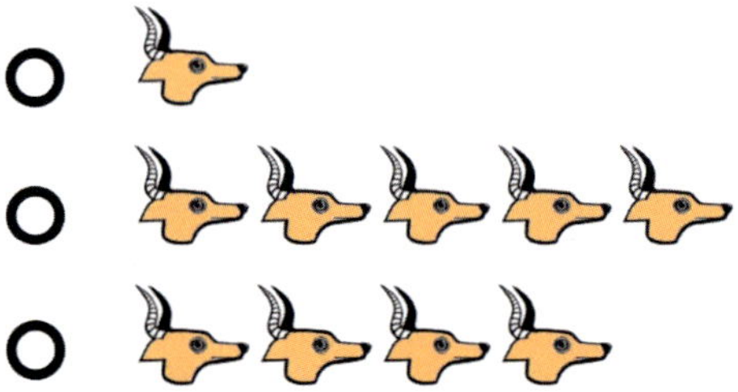

Which group shows 2 creatures?

Which group shows 3 bears?

Which group shows 5 creatures?

Which group shows 5 creatures?

Which group shows 1 creature?

Which group shows 2 creatures?

MONDAY – TUESDAY – WEDNESDAY – THURSDAY – FRIDAY – SATURDAY – SUNDAY

Missing Days #4

Write the missing days in the blank spaces provided.

1. Sunday Monday ______________

2. Wednesday Thursday ______________

3. ______________ Wednesday Thursday

4. Friday ______________ Sunday

5. Sunday ______________ Tuesday

Find the Spy #4

Find the spy by coloring the spaces with the following characters: The 1st one is done for you. Use your favorite colors!

Once you have colored all the above character's spaces, the remaining character left in the grid is the spy! Circle the spy from the 3 choices at the bottom of the page, and then color the spy!

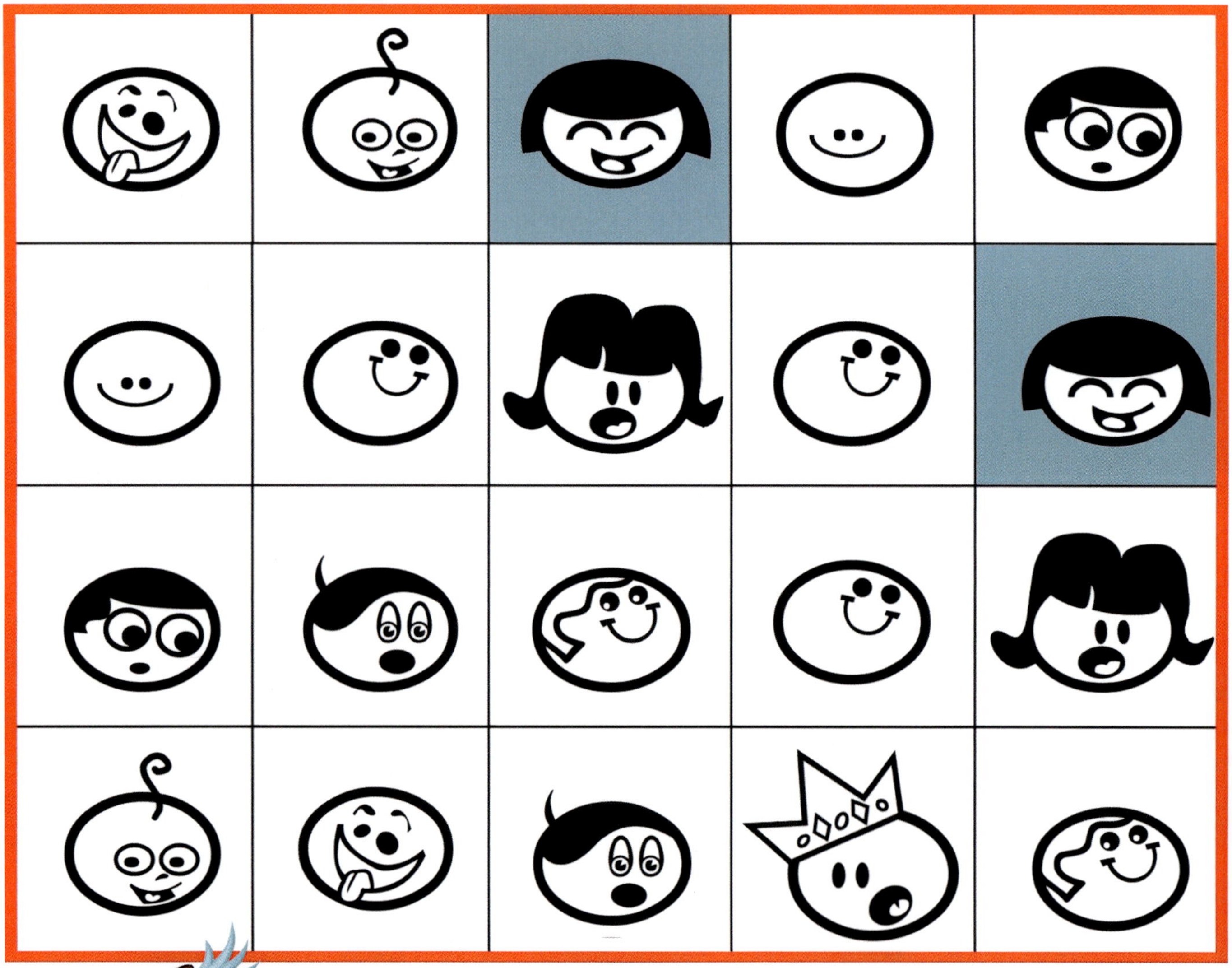

Circle the Spy:

Teaching Time #4

Look at the clock. What time is it? Color in the circle next to the correct answer.

11:00	6:00	8:00	2:00
○	○	○	○

4:00	10:00	9:00	8:00
○	○	○	○

9:00	7:00	6:00	11:00
○	○	○	○

9:00	10:00	5:00	6:00
○	○	○	○

Disorder and Disarray #4

Take a careful look at these two sets of characters. Each side has a character that is not on the other side. Color the **matching** characters—even though they may be different sizes—and find the **unique** characters that are on each side!

Hide and Seek #4

Look for the flower style in the **"Find This"** box. Then look in the **"How Many?"** box for how many to find in the series below. Color the flowers **GREEN** when you find them! The 1st one is done for you. Look carefully—some of the flowers can look similar.

Find This	How Many?
	8

SHADOW MATCHING:

Put the shadow's number on the line beneath the matching flowers and farm animals! The 1st one is done for you as an example.

5

1 2 3 4

Shadow Matching Game

Write the letter of the matching shadow on the line provided!

a b c d

a b c d

Start by crossing off each of the pictures when you find that it has a matching one!
FIND ONE PICTURE WITHOUT A COPY

Alphabet Letters # 5

Fill in the blank next to the "lower case" letter on the left side caterpillar with its matching "upper case" letter you will find on the right side caterpillar. The first one is done for you.

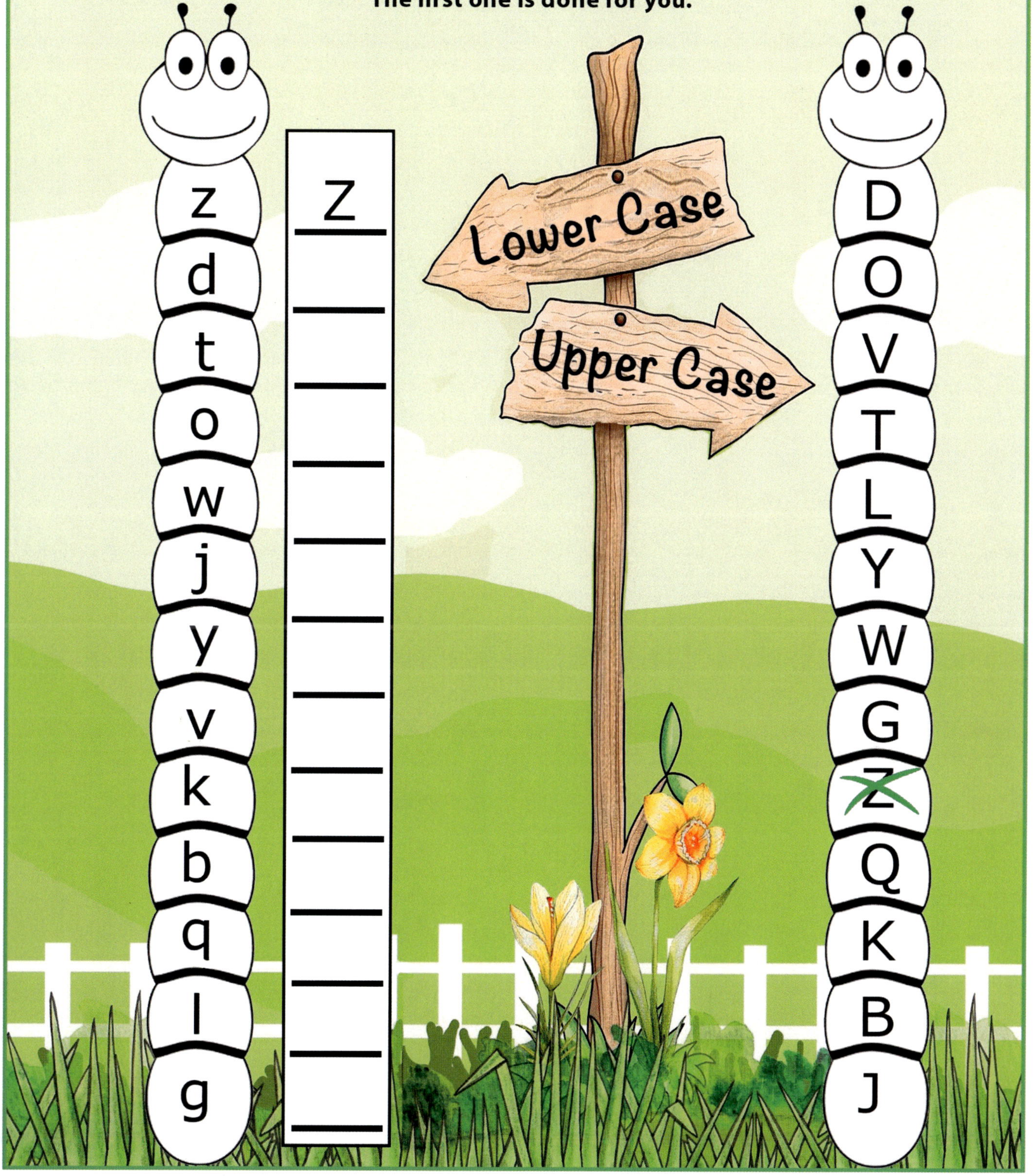

Counting Fun #5

Read each question and color the circle next to the correct answer.

Which group shows 6 pigs?

Which group shows 1 creature?

Which group shows 5 cows?

Which group shows 1 panda?

Which group shows 5 horses?

Which group shows 1 creature?

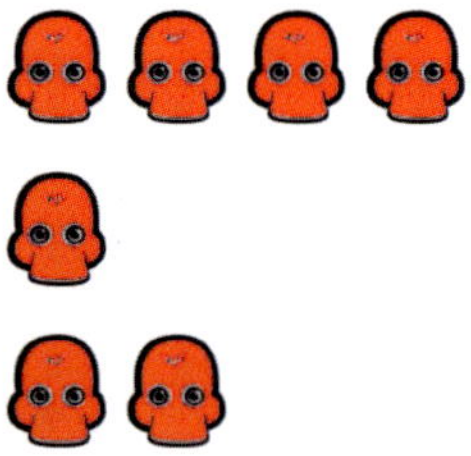

Which group shows 4 creatures?

Which group shows 4 cows?

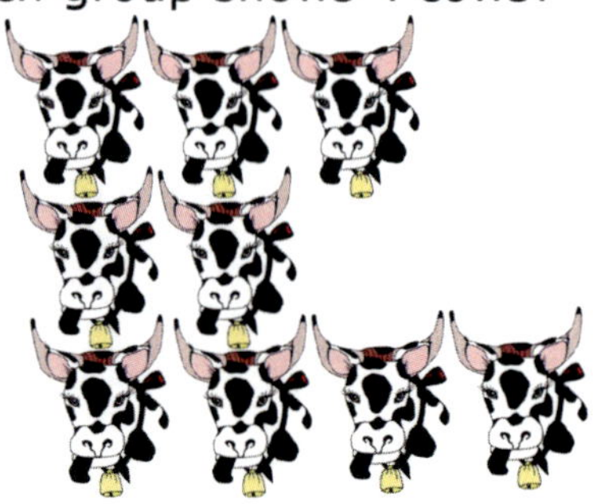

MONDAY – TUESDAY – WEDNESDAY – THURSDAY – FRIDAY – SATURDAY – SUNDAY

Missing Days #5

Write the missing days in the blank spaces provided.

1. Monday ________ Wednesday

2. Monday Tuesday ________

3. ________ Saturday Sunday

4. Wednesday ________ Friday

5. Monday ________ Wednesday

Find the Spy #5

Find the spy by coloring the spaces with the following characters: The 1st one is done for you. Use your favorite colors!

Once you have colored all the above character's spaces, the remaining character left in the grid is the spy! Circle the spy from the 3 choices at the bottom of the page, and then color the spy!

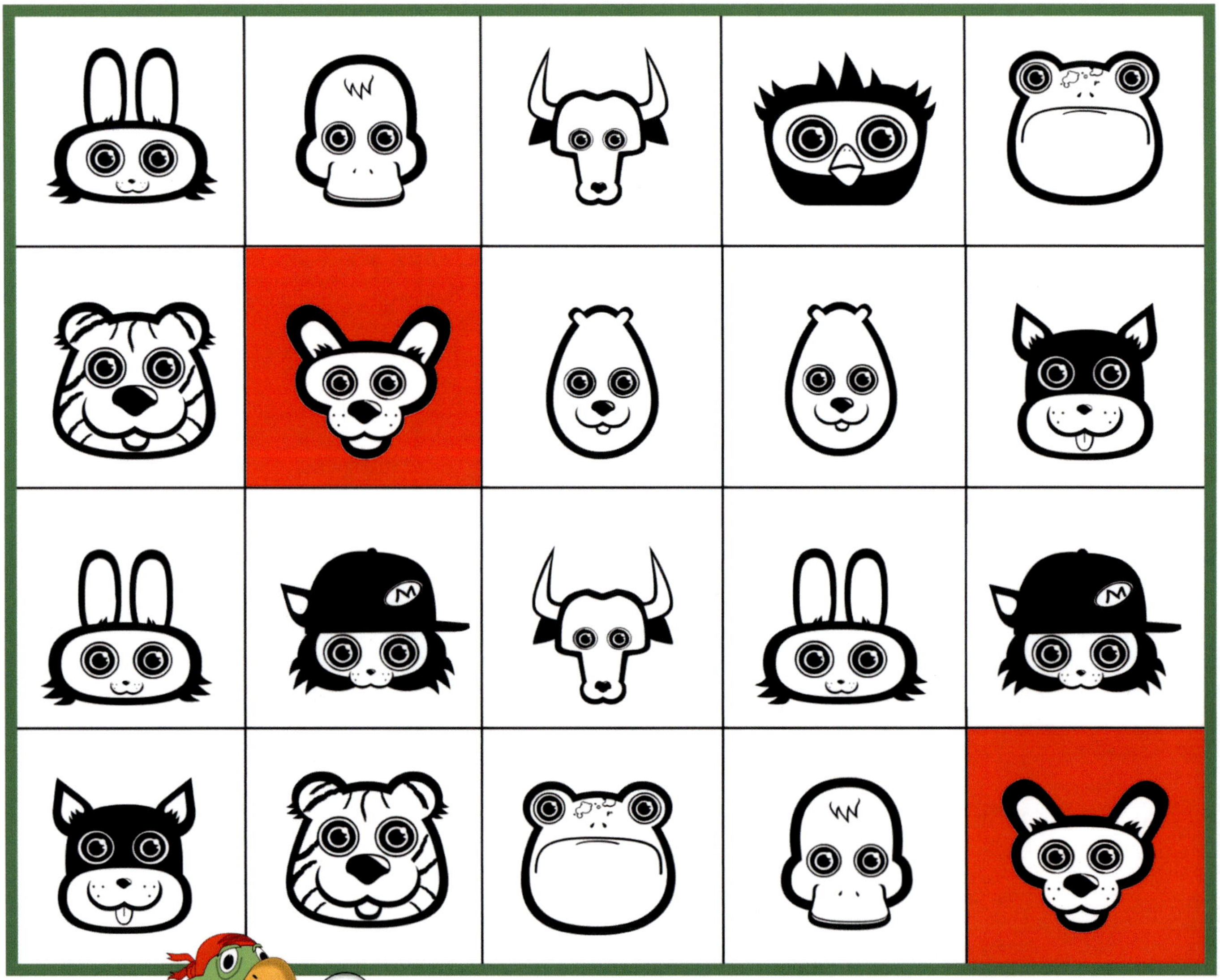

Circle the Spy:

Teaching Time #5

Look at the clock. What time is it? Color in the circle next to the correct answer.

6:00 ○	4:00 ○	7:00 ○	1:00 ○

3:00 ○	9:00 ○	2:00 ○	5:00 ○

9:30 ○	5:30 ○	10:30 ○	2:30 ○

12:00 ○	10:00 ○	4:00 ○	8:00 ○

Disorder and Disarray #5

Take a careful look at these two sets of characters. Each side has a character that is not on the other side. Color the **matching** characters—even though they may be different sizes—and find the **unique** characters that are on each side!

Hide and Seek #5

Look for the flower style in the **"Find This"** box. Then look in the **"How Many?"** box for how many to find in the series below. Color the flowers **PURPLE** when you find them! The 1st one is done for you. Look carefully—some of the flowers can look similar.

Find This

How Many?

5

Draw a line from dot number 1 to dot number 2, then from dot number 2 to dot number 3, then dot 3 to 4, and so on. Continue to join the dots until you have connected all the numbered dots. Then color the rest of the picture!

SOLUTIONS

Alphabet Letters

#1 (Page 5): I, E, A, G, M, R, N, D, Z, J, S, H, O

#2 (Page 13): B, E, S, C, I, P, O, A, L, R, G, U, Q

#3 (Page 21): U, I, V, M, Q, X, S, F, A, R, E, Y, D

#4 (Page 29): R, E, A, Z, G, I, U, K, O, X, L, V, S

#5 (Page 39): Z, D, T, O, W, J, Y, V, K, B, Q, L, G

Counting Fun: # 1 - #5

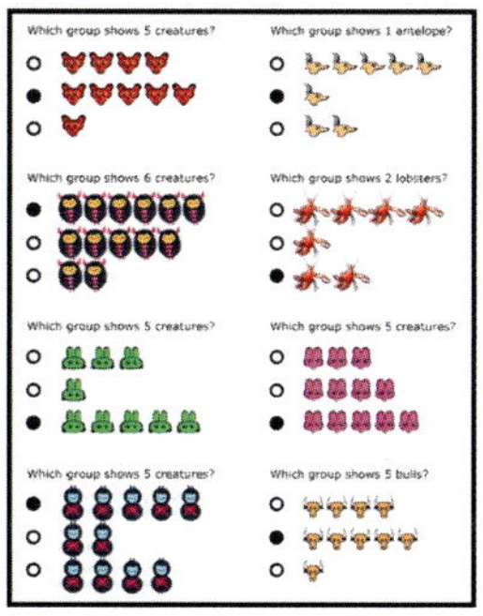

Page 6

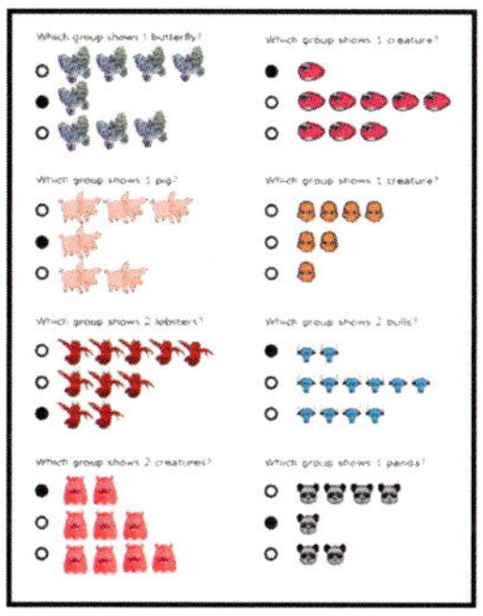

Page 14

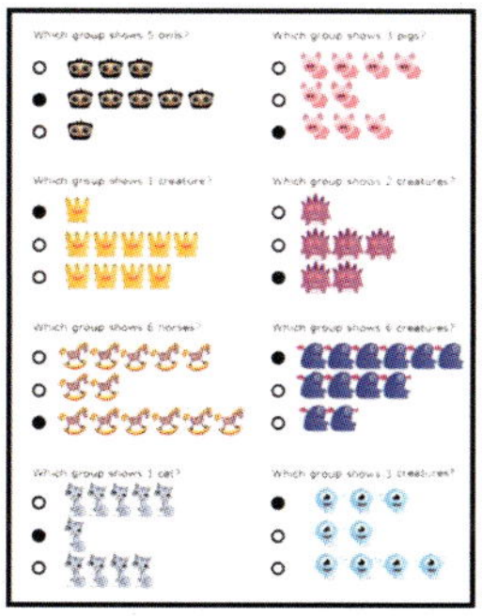

Page 22

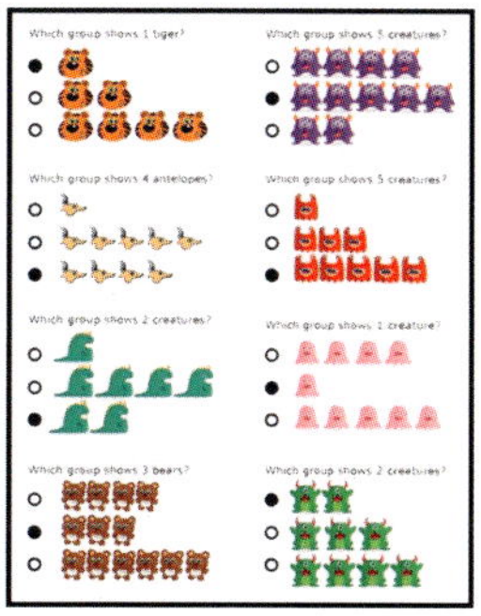

Page 30

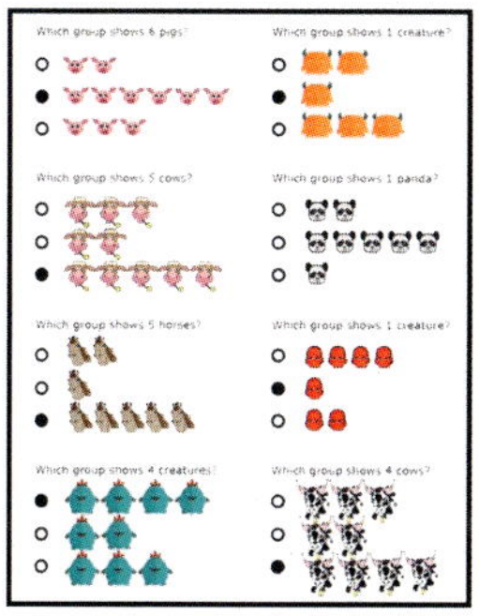

Page 40

Missing Days

#1 Page 7): Monday, Saturday, Tuesday, Thursday, Friday

#2 (Page 15): Friday, Wednesday, Sunday, Friday, Monday

#3 (Page 23): Monday, Thursday, Tuesday, Friday, Sunday

#4 (Page 31): Tuesday, Friday, Tuesday, Saturday, Monday

#5 (Page 41): Tuesday, Wednesday, Friday, Thursday, Tuesday

Find the Spy

#1 (Page 8)

#2 (Page 16)

#3 (Page 24)

#4 (Page 32)

#5 (Page 42)

Teaching Time

#1 (Page 9): 11:00, 9:00, 3:00, 12:00

#2 (Page 17): 5:00, 4:30, 7:00, 8:15

#3 (Page 25): 3:15, 6:30, 2:30, 9:15

#4 (Page 33): 2:00, 4:00, 7:00, 10:00

#5 (Page 43): 6:00, 3:00, 10:30, 12:00

SOLUTIONS (continued)

Disorder and Disarray

#1 (Page 10)
Left Right

#2 (Page18)
Left Right

#3 (Page 26)
Left Right

#4 (Page 34)
Left Right

#5 (Page 44)
Left Right

Hide and Seek

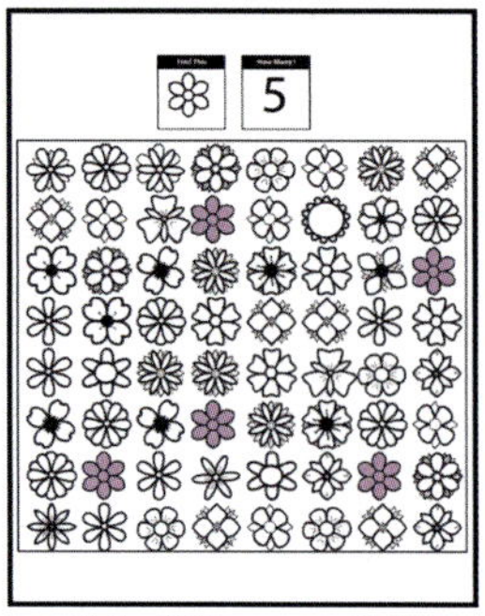

#1 (Page 11)

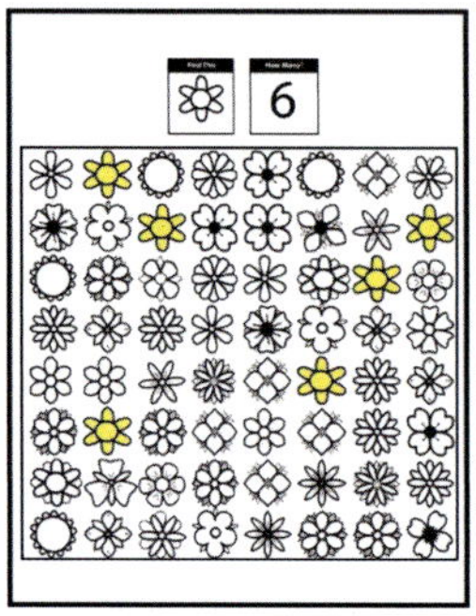

#2 (Page 19)

#3 (Page 27)

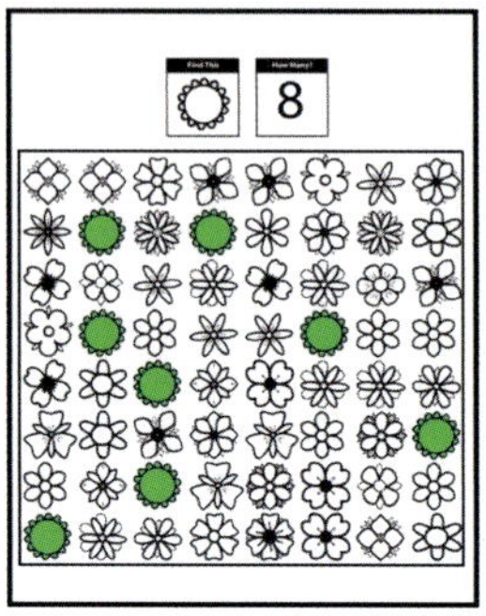

#4 (Page 35)

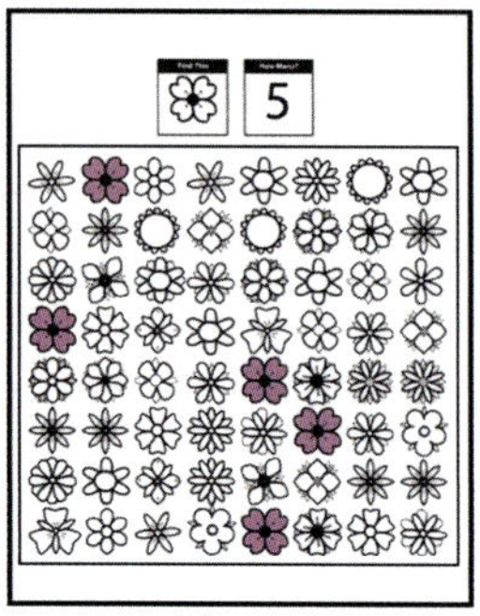

#5 (Page 45)

MATCH THE NUMBER to the number's name!

Page 12

WHAT DOES NOT FIT? Circle the one that's different

Page 20

Match the Colors

Page 28

Shadow Matching

Page 36

Shadow Matching

Page 37

Find One Picture

Page 38

Dot-to-Dot

Page 46

Other books available by Dorothy-Frances Books:
Available on Amazon.com
dfbooks.com

Creative Coloring® Series: Coloring Journals/Seasons

These coloring journals each have events that happen around the world in that book's season and inspirational sayings throughout the book; journal prompts are also part of this series.

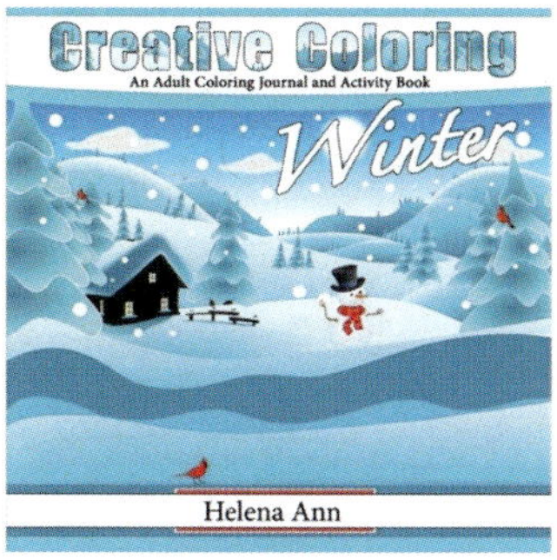

Easter: A beautiful "grayscale" coloring book with inspirational quotes and Biblical passages.

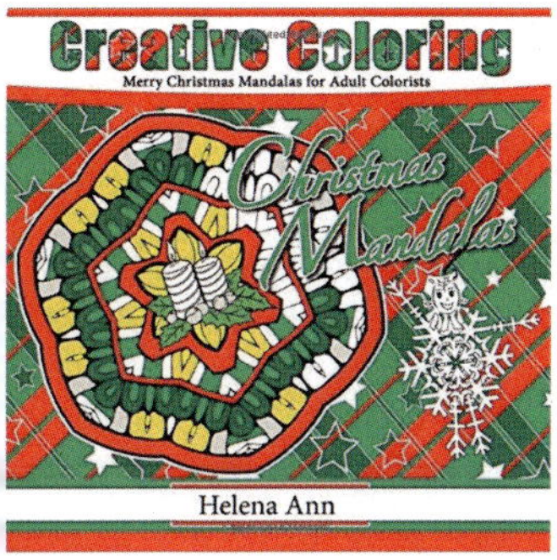

Christmas: 30 Christmas-themed mandalas and designs, including designs of the *Twelve Days of Christmas*.

Other books available by Dorothy-Frances Books:
Available on Amazon.com
dfbooks.com

A to Z Animals: A kid's Animal Coloring and Puzzle book. Big or small, domestic or wild, animals make our lives awesome. All puzzles have elements to color and there are fun animal facts, too! Many types of puzzles are included, especially fun are the Tangram puzzles!

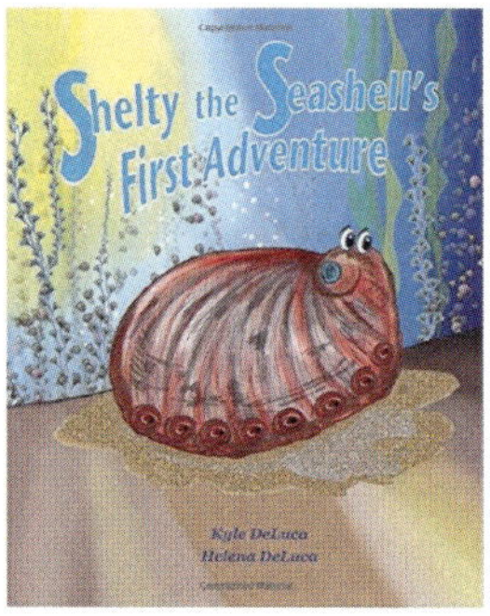

Shelty the Seashell's First Adventure: this is a transitional chapter book for the early reader. Short chapters that can also be a great book for an older brother or sister to read to a younger child. Shelty encounters an angry starfish and squid before he comes in contact with the scary sea monster . . . or is he really scary?

Creative Doodle Design series: 1) Steampunk designs/story, 2) Valentine's Day

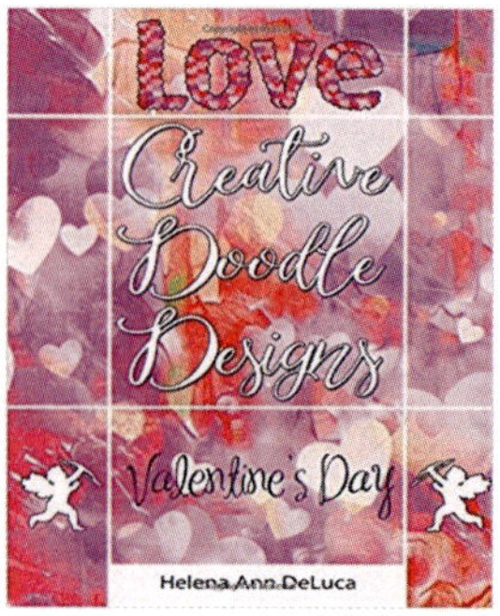

Sharpen Your Pencil . . . Sharpen Your Brain series:

Florida: Word Search and other puzzles that all have a Florida theme. Also, learn about the many different places to visit in Florida.

Made in the USA
Columbia, SC
30 June 2020

12978269R00029